How often have you had great ideas forget about them when you get hom help you get a step closer to your dre business or for your life?

Do you have a million ideas floating in your head that you need to get down on paper or maybe you just have to brainstorm that content idea out and do some mind maps?

This A5 book is the perfect size with a unique design and will fit in your bag. It is super light weight and easy to carry everywhere. You also get inside, pages to plan what and who you want to be, do & have in life. A page to plan your ideal day and then you can complete the five pages of goal planning questions to help you brainstorm and clarify at least one major goal for your business this year. The rest of the book contains lots of space for your notes and mind maps!

Now, follow the steps below to help you reach your goals…

1. Think of something you want to do or work towards. What are your interests - how could you incorporate what you like into a big goal? (use the following worksheets to help you)
2. Write them down in your notebook.
3. Tell someone. Telling someone we know about our goals also seems to increase the likelihood that we will stick at them.
4. Break your goal down into steps, this will become your actionable plan. This is especially important for big goals.
5. Take action on your first step.
6. Keep going - rinse and repeat.
7. Celebrate, then keep writing and creating new goals, never settle for just one!

Copyright ©2020 by Sharon Howat.
All rights reserved. This book or any portion thereof may not be reproduced or used in any manner whatsoever without the express written permission of the publisher except for the use of brief quotations in a book review or scholarly journal.
First Printing:2020

www.sharonhowat.com
Why not tag me in your stories over on Instagram @sharon.howat

Be, Do, Have

EVERYTHING IS CREATED TWICE.
FIRST IN THE MIND & THEN IN REALITY!

Create a list of everything you want to BE.
Everything you want to DO and
Everything you want to HAVE.

Written on:

BE	DO	HAVE

Fill it out and keep looking at it.
Use this as a visual reminder to keep you heading in the right direction.

My Ideal Day

DESCRIBE IN DETAIL, YOUR IDEAL DAY

*How and where do you wake up? Where do you live?
Who lives with you? How do you spend your morning?
What do you eat? What do you do first?
How do you spend your time?
What are you excited about doing today?*

Written on:

This is how my day goes...

This is how my day goes...

My Big Goals & My Little Goals...

MAKE A LIST OF YOUR TOP 50+ GOALS

No matter how big and small, list everything you want to be able to do, be it every day, once a week, once a month and even once a year.

Written on:

These are the things I want to be able to do & buy and will do what it takes to get them...

1)	10)
2)	11)
3)	12)
4)	12)
5)	14)
6)	15)
7)	16)
8)	17)
9)	18)

19)	37)
20)	38)
21)	39)
22)	40)
23)	41)
24)	42)
25)	43)
26)	44)
27)	45)
28)	46)
29)	47)
30)	48)
31)	49)
32)	50)
33)	51)
34)	52)
35)	53)
36)	54)

One Main Goal

	Your Answers
What is the one big goal I want to achieve for my business this year?	I want to Date I wish to achieve this by: __/__/20__
What would I love to do more of in my business this year? (What energises me and makes work feel like fun?)	I would really like to… I love…
Which part of my business would I like to get rid of?	

What would I like to add to my business this year?	My own eBook on Kindle Increase Products Promotions Webinars Facebook Live Events Videos & YouTube Podcasts A membership site Create an event Mentoring or coaching VIP options Other_____
What changes did I make last year that proved beneficial to my business? What one change could I make right now that will: Save me time Reduce stress Move me closer to my big goal Increase visibility Other	

What do you do well that will move you towards your goal? How will it further your goal?	
What do you need to outsource? (graphic creation, scheduling posts etc)	
Have you set a budget for this year? How does your goal fit into your budget? (Will you need to generate extra cash?)	
How much income do you need to achieve your big goal?	£ _____

Is this my goal or is someone or something else pressuring me to achieve it?	
What will achieving this goal do…	☐ For me ☐ For my business ☐ For my community ☐ For my subscribers ☐ For my family
How can I tweak this goal so that it feels even better and gives back more?	

Do I have all the equipment/software or services I need to comfortably meet this goal? (laptop, computer, printer, phone camera quality for creating my own photo shoots etc)	
What do I still have to acquire?	
Is anything stopping me from acquiring the item/person I need? If so, how can I get past this block?	

How I plan to achieve my goals...

Mind Maps – Let's Think Deeper

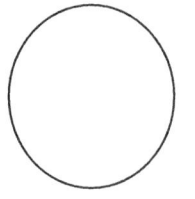

○

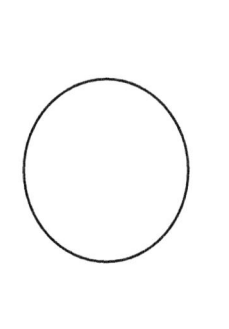

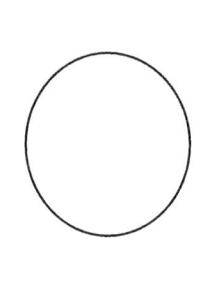

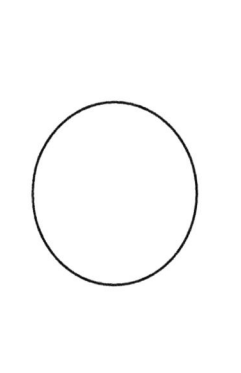

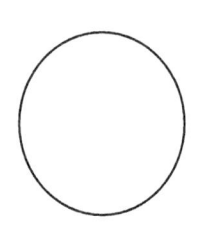

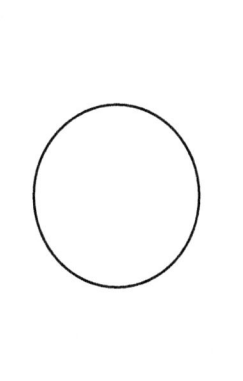

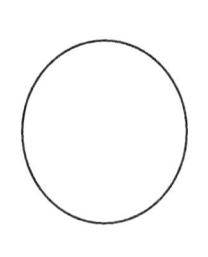

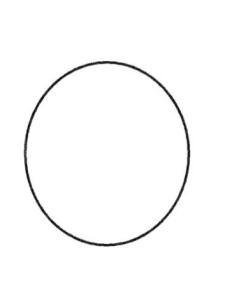

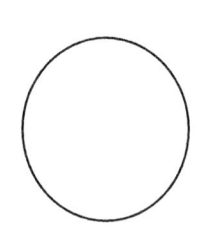

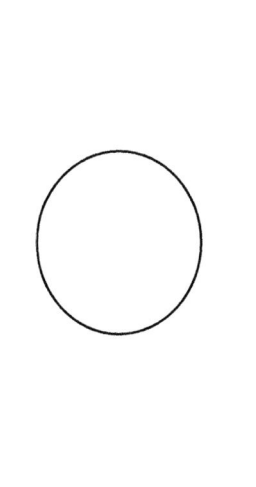

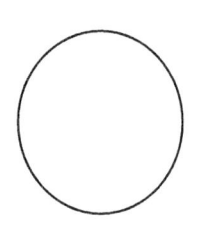

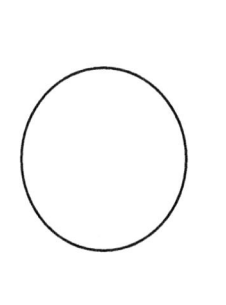

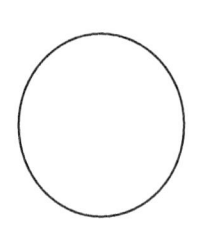

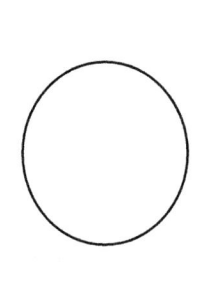

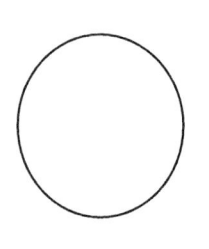

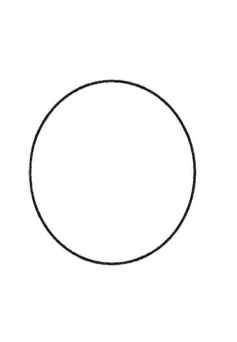

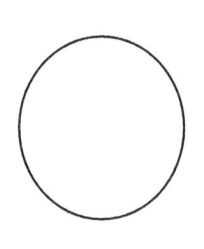

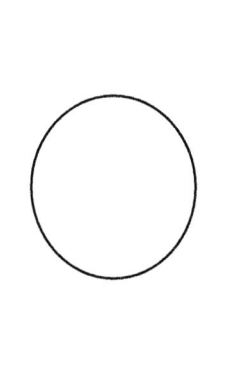

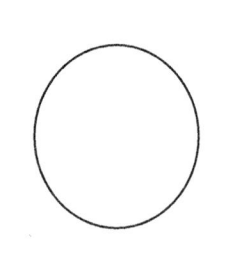

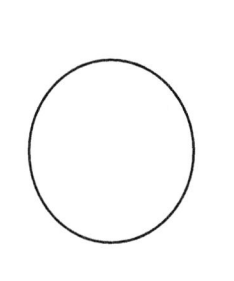

Printed in Great Britain
by Amazon